11,777

Carlson, Bernice (Wells)

Funny-bone dramatics. Illustrated by Charles Cox. Nashville, Abingdon press, [1974]

96p. illus.

bibliography: p.93-94

1.Children's plays. 2.Wit and humor. 3.Plays. 4.Riddles. I.Title.

Funny-Bone Dramatics

Funny-Bone Dramatics

Bernice Wells Carlson

Illustrated by
Charles Cox

ABINGDON PRESS
NASHVILLE NEW YORK

FUNNY-BONE DRAMATICS

Printed in the United States of America

Library of Congress Cataloguing in Publication Data

CARLSON, BERNICE (WELLS)

Funny-bone dramatics.

SUMMARY: A selection of humorous riddles, plays, and puppet jokes with directions for presenting them to an audience.

Bibliography: p.

1. Children's plays. 2. Wit and humor, Juvenile. 1. Plays. 2. Riddles. I. Title.

PN6120.H803 812'.5'4 73-21515

ISBN 0-687-13867-1

To
Carol
and
Katherine

Contents

Introduction

To tickle a funny bone can mean one of two things. It can mean to touch a certain sensitive spot on the elbow, or it can mean to make someone laugh. So, funny-bone dramatics may include any kind of acting that makes someone laugh.

In this book you'll find four kinds of funny-bone dramatics:

1. speak-up riddles to ask a friend or group
2. jokes that are told and, to a certain extent, acted out by puppets
3. skits that are dramatized jokes with comic characters as actors
4. plays that are dramatized stories about people who act in a silly way

The material in this book is arranged from the most simple kind of activity to the more complicated. Start with something easy. Ask your family a riddle. Or, using a puppet in each hand, act out a puppet joke. Then work with another person or with a group of people to act out a puppet joke or to put on a skit or play.

FUNNY-BONE DRAMATICS

These dramatic activities are short. You can use one or two as part of a program in school, at camp, Brownie or Cub Scout meetings, or any other group gathering.

You can present a program with different kinds of funny-bone dramatics.

You can act out puppet jokes at home or when playing with neighborhood friends. You can also think of other ways to use the material in this book.

No matter how you use these funny-bone dramatics, have fun! Remember that everyone has a funny bone. Tickle it!

Speak-Up Riddles

Riddles often have funny and unexpected answers. If you learn to ask a riddle well, you'll develop the ability to speak clearly and loudly enough for listeners to hear and understand each word you say.

A comic actor must learn to put his lines across, that is, to speak so that everyone can understand him. Asking riddles before a group can help you develop this art.

Riddles

What kind of snakes are like baby's toys?

❧ Rattlers.

What kind of coat is put on wet and has no buttons?
☙ A coat of paint.

What gets wetter as it dries?
☙ A towel.

Why is a river like a dollar bill?
☙ Because it goes from bank to bank.

What starts with *t*, ends with *t*, and has *t* in it?
☙ A teapot.

Why do snowflakes dance?
☙ Because they are getting ready for a snowball.

Why is the ocean restless?
☙ Because it has rocks in its bed.

If you were facing east, what would be on your left hand?
☙ Fingers.

Why is a river so rich?
☙ Because it has two banks.

What has a face and hands but no body or legs?
☙ A clock.

On what side of a pitcher is the handle?
On the outside.

What travels all over the United States and still stays in one corner?
A postage stamp.

What question can never be answered by yes?
Are you asleep?

What is lower with a head than without one?
A pillow.

Why did the greenhouse call the doctor?
It was full of panes.

What would happen to a white stone if you threw it into the Red Sea?
It would get wet.

Funny-Bone
Puppet Jokes

A dramatic joke is a special kind of joke. The teller, whether he is a puppet or a person, pretends to be someone else by imitating the voice and manner of speaking of a particular character.

In the following puppet jokes, two or more puppets talk to each other or ask questions. You can use a puppet in each hand. Or, two or more people can take part in the act, each working a puppet.

You can use any kind of puppet, but do not use a puppet theater or hide behind a screen. Tell your puppet jokes directly to your listeners, and at the same time remember to imitate the voice of each character and make each puppet bob up and down or sway back and forth at the right time.

In most cases the names of the puppets are unimportant. The speakers could be boys or girls, men or women. Change the names if you wish.

Before you start to dramatize a joke, study it. Some lines are *filler* lines, such as "Good morning," "How are you?" and so on.

This type of line helps the audience identify each character and sets the stage for the joke. Say them in your own words if you wish.

In every joke, however, there are one or two very important lines. One is the *lead* line that builds up to the joke. The other is the *punch* line that makes the joke funny. The humor of the joke usually depends on the exact wording of these lines. Pick them out and learn them exactly.

When you present a funny-bone puppet joke, say the filler lines quickly. Make the puppets bob their heads up and down and move their bodies. But, when you come to the lead line and the punch line, say these lines slowly, clearly, and loudly. You must help the audience understand every word of these lines. After the punch line, make the puppets laugh and laugh with their heads bobbing up and down and their bodies swaying back and forth.

Ginger

Characters

TIMMY AUNT EMMA

AUNT EMMA: You have a nice dog, Timmy.

TIMMY (*nodding*): Mmm-hmmm.

AUNT EMMA: What's her name?

TIMMY: Ginger.

AUNT EMMA: Does Ginger bite?

TIMMY: Oh, no!

AUNT EMMA: That's nice.

TIMMY: Ginger doesn't bite. Ginger snaps!

For the Tour

Characters

MR. BLIMP, a tourist TOUR GUIDE
Other tourists if you wish

MR. BLIMP: Thank you for the guided tour of the city.

GUIDE: You are welcome, sir.

(*If there are other tourists, they nod, saying* "Thank you" *softly.*)

MR. BLIMP: You seem to know the city very well.

GUIDE: Yes, sir. I know every part of this city.

MR. BLIMP: Have you lived here all your life?

GUIDE: Not yet, sir.

A Cup of Tea

Characters

MRS. FINNEY MRS. NUTTY

MRS. FINNEY: Good morning, Mrs. Nutty.

MRS. NUTTY: Good morning, Mrs. Finney.

MRS. FINNEY: I'm so glad you came.

MRS. NUTTY: I wanted to come.

MRS. FINNEY: Can you stay a little bit?

MRS. NUTTY: Oh, yes, I can stay a little bit.

MRS. FINNEY: Will you join me in a cup of tea?

MRS. NUTTY: Oh, I'm sorry. I don't think there's room for both of us *in* a cup of tea.

Rope Joke

Characters

SLIM TIM JIM

(SLIM *and* TIM *put their heads together for a moment then laugh and laugh.* "Ho! Ho! Ho!" *They put their heads together again, listen a moment, then laugh and laugh.*

JIM *watches, leans forward trying to hear, can't understand, feels left out.*)

JIM: What are you two laughing at?

SLIM: We're telling jokes.

JIM: I like jokes.

SLIM: We like our jokes.

TIM: We know your jokes.

JIM: Did you ever hear the rope joke?

SLIM *and* TIM: No.

SLIM: Tell us the the rope joke.

JIM: Skip it!

Freight Goes By

Characters

SAM BAM

(*Puppets sway back and forth as they watch freight cars go by.*)

SAM: Tank car.

BAM: Oil.

SAM: Flat car.

BAM: Cars.

SAM: Stock car.

BAM: Cows.

SAM: Refrigerator car.

BAM: Fruit.

SAM: Box car.

BAM: Boxes.

(*Puppets stop moving.*)

SAM: Say, Bam, what kind of train carries bubble gum?

BAM: That's easy, Sam. A chew-chew train carries bubble gum.

A Piece?

Characters

STEPHEN SALESMAN

(STEPHEN'S *head bobs up and down as if he is looking at a cage. He moves as if looking at another cage.*)

SALESMAN: Good morning. Can I help you?

STEPHEN: I want to buy a puppy.

SALESMAN: Good.

STEPHEN: How much are they?

SALESMAN: Ten dollars apiece.

STEPHEN: Ten dollars a piece?

SALESMAN: Yes.

STEPHEN: But I want to buy a whole puppy. I don't want a piece!

Birthday Candles

Characters

MOM SALLY

SALLY: Hi, Mom!

MOM: Hi, Sally. Did you have a good time at the birthday party?

SALLY: Mmm-hmmm!

MOM: What did you do?

SALLY: I played games.

MOM: That's nice.

SALLY: I got a hat.

MOM: That's nice.

SALLY: I had a lot of food.

MOM: That's nice.

SALLY: And I found out what one birthday candle says to another birthday candle.

MOM: What does one birthday candle say to another birthday candle?

SALLY: It says, "These birthday parties burn me up!"

Smart Dog

Characters

MR. KENNEDY GREGG SNOOP

MR. KENNEDY: That's a nice dog you have.

GREGG: Thank you. He's nice and he's smart.

SNOOP: Arf!

MR. KENNEDY: A smart dog. What's his name?

GREGG: Snoop.

SNOOP: Arf!

MR. KENNEDY: Hello, Snoop. What kind of dog do you think he is?

GREGG: A police dog.

SNOOP: Arf!

MR. KENNEDY: A police dog? He doesn't look like a police dog!

GREGG: Of course he doesn't. He's a police detective in disguise.

SNOOP: Arf!

Wrong Answer

Characters

GIANT GHOST

FAIRY IMP

(*Use stick puppets.*)

GIANT (*in giant voice*): Where is Imp?

FAIRY (*in gentle voice*): He's gone to human school.

GHOST (*in spooky voice*): Poor Imp. He has a hard time with human words. Here he comes now.

(IMP *appears.*)

GIANT, FAIRY, GHOST: Hi, Imp!

IMP (*sadly*): Hi.

GIANT: How did it go in human school?

IMP: Badly. Teacher said I got the wrong answer. What is a wrong answer?

GIANT: A wrong answer is an error.

FAIRY: A wrong answer is a mistake.

IMP: Ghost, what do you call a wrong answer?

GHOST (*in slow clear voice*): I say a wrong answer is a boo-boo!

See Mom!

Characters

GABBY MOM

MOM: Gabby, Baby's sick. I can't take you to the dentist's.

GABBY: I can go alone, Mom. Honest, I can go alone. Let me go alone, Mom.

MOM: OK, Gabby. You may go alone. But remember, don't talk all the time. Learn to shut your mouth.

GABBY: I won't talk all the time, Mom. Honest, I'll shut my mouth. (*Keeps talking.*)

MOM: Gabby, get going! Remember, don't talk all the time. Good-bye.

GABBY: Good-bye, Mom. I'll remember, Mom. (*Both exit.*)

(*An hour later.*)

MOM: Hi, Gabby! How did it go at the dentist's?

GABBY: Great, Mom.

MOM: Did you talk all the time?

GABBY: No, Mom, I didn't open my mouth.

MOM: What? You didn't open your mouth at the dentist's?

GABBY: That's right, Mom. I didn't open my mouth at the dentist's. (*Puts head forward.*) See. No fillings!

Noah's Ark

Characters

BUFFY STUFFY

(BUFFY *and* STUFFY *are swaying back and forth, singing to the tune of* "Here We Go Round the Mountain, Two by Two." *If you don't know the tune, chant the verse.*)

BUFFY *and* STUFFY: The animals went marching, two by two.
The animals went marching, two by two.
The animals went marching, two by two
Into Noah's ark.

BUFFY: Say, Stuffy, what animal took the most luggage into Noah's ark?

STUFFY: Let me think. What animal took the most luggage into Noah's ark? I don't know. I give up.

BUFFY: The elephant. He took his trunk.

STUFFY: That's right. Now let me ask you something. What animal took the least luggage into Noah's ark?

STUFFY: What animal took the least luggage into Noah's ark? I don't know. I give up.

BUFFY: The rooster. He took his comb.

Thank You

Characters

MOM ELLEN

ELLEN: Hi, Mom!

MOM: Hi, Ellen. Did you have a nice time at Susie's party?

ELLEN: Oh, yes!

MOM: Did you play games?

ELLEN: Oh, yes.

MOM: Did you like the food?

ELLEN: Oh, yes.

MOM: Did you thank Susie's mother for the good time when you said "good-bye"?

ELLEN: No, I didn't.

MOM: You didn't thank Mrs. Kelly? Why not?

ELLEN: I listened to Kate O'Fallon.

MOM: You listened to Kate O'Fallon? So what?

ELLEN: Kate said, "Thank you, Mrs. Kelly, for the nice time." Mrs. Kelly said, "Don't mention it." So I didn't mention it.

The Fly

Characters

WANDA DUANE

WANDA: Hi, Duane.

DUANE: Hi, Wanda.

WANDA: I want to ask you something.

DUANE: What?

WANDA: If a fly got in a pitcher of syrup, how would he get out?

DUANE: I don't know. I'm stuck.

WANDA: So's the fly.

Lost Dog

Characters

MR. TOTH JANIE

(JANIE *is crying out loud.*)

JANIE: Boohoohoo!

MR. TOTH: There, there, little girl. Don't cry.

(JANIE *continues to cry out loud.*)

MR. TOTH: Why are you crying?

JANIE: I lost my dog.

MR. TOTH: Maybe he'll come home.

JANIE: No, he won't come home. He's lost!

MR. TOTH: Did you put a lost ad in the paper?

JANIE: No, it wouldn't do any good to put a lost ad in the paper.

MR. TOTH: Why not?

JANIE: My dog can't read.

Good for What?

Characters

SETH DAD

SETH: Hi, Dad! Are you busy?

DAD: Not really. What do you want?

SETH: A dime. Dad, will you give me a dime?

DAD: I don't know about that.

SETH: Please, Dad! I'll be real good.

DAD: You'll be real good for a dime?

SETH (*nodding*): Mmm-hmmm.

DAD: Well, of all things! When I was your age, I was good for nothing!

Funny-Bone Skits

Funny-bone skits are acted-out jokes or funny situations. Like all skits, they are short. You must get the idea across quickly.

In every funny-bone skit there is a punch line, the line that makes the skit funny. Before you start to plan a skit, read it carefully and pick out this line.

Every actor in a skit must be ready for a punch line. The actor who says it must memorize this line exactly and then say it clearly, slowly, and loudly. The audience must be able to understand every word.

If other actors are onstage, they must listen for the punch line, pay attention to the speaker, and then react to his remark. They may choose how they would react and then end the skit as they wish.

A few hints may help a punch-line speaker get these lines across:
—Stand as close to the audience as possible.
—Face the audience directly.
—If the audience laughs, pause a moment without dropping out of character, then go on with lines and action.

The characters in a skit are not like real people. Everything that they say and do is exaggerated. As an actor, exaggerate your motions and emotional reactions. Move your arms more freely, laugh harder, or cry harder than you would do normally. React to a joke or disaster with your entire body. In other words: throw yourself into the part and let yourself go!

The stage can be any area large enough to allow actors to move about—the front of a classroom, a portion of a meeting room or gym, part of a living room at home, or a grassy spot at camp.

You don't need a curtain. Two persons with signs marked "curtain" may stand in the center of the acting area. When it is time for the skit to start, they part and walk in opposite directions to the sides of the "stage." At the end of the skit, they come together.

An announcer may describe a scene. Or someone may hold up a sign telling where the action takes place.

Don't worry about scenery. Label a box or table "refrigerator" or a chair "camel" if the script calls for them.

Costumes aren't necessary. Forget them, unless you enjoy making paper hats, or draping sheets in special ways, or pulling old clothes from closets and trunks and dressing up in them.

Spend your time and energy on the skit itself, on the acting, and on the timing of the lines. Have fun being a funny-bone actor.

Nothing!

Characters

RICH BABYSITTER
ROBIN

SCENE. *The kitchen. A table is placed center front. On it is a small cookie jar with a lid.*

(ROBIN *and* RICH *are chewing.* ROBIN *lifts lid of cookie jar.*)

ROBIN: They're gone!

(RICH *looks in.*)

RICH: All gone.

ROBIN: We didn't eat many.

RICH: Not very many.

ROBIN: There must be more.

RICH: She always bakes more.

ROBIN: Bet the babysitter hid them.

RICH: I bet. But where?

ROBIN: Let's look.

(*They pantomime thinking about a good place, looking, finding nothing, thinking again, more looking. Babysitter enters unnoticed, stands staring, then speaks.*)

BABYSITTER: What are you two looking for?

ROBIN: Nothing.

RICH: Nothing.

BABYSITTER: Nothing?

ROBIN: Honest, nothing.

RICH: Nothing.

BABYSITTER: Oh, nothing! I bet you'll find nothing in that cookie jar. (*Points to jar.*)

What do Robin and Rich do? Look in the jar and pretend to be surprised? Laugh and leave the kitchen? Or what? You decide.

Make Your Own Bed

Characters

CLERK SALESMAN

SCENE. *Office of Save-a-Mint Motel.* CLERK *stands behind a desk placed center stage. The desk is large enough to conceal boards, saw, hammer, and can of nails. A large carton, or matching cartons can be used for a desk. On top of the desk is a notebook for registering guests and a pen.*

(SALESMAN *carrying suitcase enters.* CLERK *steps in front of desk to greet him.*)

CLERK: Welcome to Save-a-Mint Motel. Can I help you?

SALESMAN: I hope so. I need a good but cheap room for a few days.

CLERK: We have the right room for you—clean, airy, and low-priced.

SALESMAN: How can you charge less than the Gerald Grand Motel down the road?

CLERK: We cut services not quality of rooms.

SALESMAN: What services do you cut?

CLERK: Will you carry your bags to your room?

SALESMAN: Yes, I'll carry my bags.

CLERK: Will you accept a room with a shower but no tub?

SALESMAN: Yes, I can use a shower.

CLERK: Will you make your own bed?

SALESMAN (*after thinking a moment*): Yes, I'll make my own bed.

CLERK: Good.

(CLERK *goes behind desk.* SALESMAN *steps forward as if he is to sign register.* CLERK *pulls, from behind desk, boards, saw, hammer, box of nails.*)

CLERK: Get busy! Make your own bed.

What does the salesman do? Pick up his bags and leave? Get mad? Start pounding? You decide.

Follow-the-Leader

Characters

HEATHER — OTHER CHILDREN
MILLIE

SCENE. *Any open space.* HEATHER *is downstage right.* MILLIE *is downstage left.*

(CHILDREN *come together happily.*)

HEATHER: Let's play follow-the-leader.

OTHER CHILDREN (*yelling*): Yes, let's!

HEATHER: I'll be leader.

(*Each points to himself and yells.*): No! I'll be leader! I'll be leader!

MILLIE (*begins to stamp and rage*): I want to be leader! I'm never leader! You won't let me be leader!

(MILLIE *continues to yell until* HEATHER *calls out.*)

HEATHER: Quiet! (*All are quiet.*) Millie's right. She's never leader. Let's make Millie leader.

OTHER CHILDREN: OK.

HEATHER: OK, Millie. You're leader.

MILLIE (*jumps up and down, claps her hands, points to herself*): Yeah! I'm leader! I'm leader!

(*Others watch her as if expecting something.*)

MILLIE (*stops and speaks soberly*): OK, I'm leader. What do we do? Where do we go?

What do the other children do? You decide.

To Play the Piano

Characters

DOCTOR NETTIE

SCENE. DOCTOR'S *office.*

(DOCTOR *is seated.* NETTIE *is standing with a big bandage around one hand.*)

DOCTOR: There you are, Nettie. Keep the bandage on your hand. Don't worry, the cut will heal.

NETTIE: Doctor, I've been wondering.

DOCTOR: About what, Nettie?

NETTIE: When my hand gets well, will I be able to play the piano?

DOCTOR: Of course, you can play the piano, Nettie.

NETTIE: That's good news! I couldn't play the piano before I cut my hand!

Home Cooking

Characters

MR. SCAT POLICEMAN

SCENE. *Street in front of a restaurant. On a cardboard or chalkboard representing the building there are two signs. The top signs says* Al's Eat House. *A lower sign says* Home Cooking.

(MR. SCAT *is standing in front of the building.* POLICEMAN *strolls onstage.*)

MR. SCAT: Pardon me. (POLICEMAN *stops and nods.*) Can you tell me where I can find a place to eat?

POLICEMAN: Right there. (*Points to building.*) Al's Eat House.

MR. SCAT: But it's closed. No one's there.

POLICEMAN: What do you mean, "Closed. No one's there"?

MR. SCAT: Read the sign, Home Cooking.

What does the policeman do? You decide.

All About Animals

Characters

JERRY GRACE

(GRACE *is reading. She turns the pages near the end of the book slowly.* JERRY *enters.*)

JERRY: Hi, Grace!

GRACE (*not looking up*): Hi, Jerry!

JERRY: Must be a good book you're reading.

GRACE: It is a good book. All about animals.

JERRY: You don't say.

GRACE (*closing book*): I have read the book. Now I know all about animals.

JERRY: OK. Then tell me what animal can jump higher than the Empire State Building.

GRACE: What animal can jump higher than the Empire State Building? I'll have to look it up. (*Glances at index.*) I don't know. What animal can jump higher than the Empire State Building?

JERRY: Any animal can jump higher than the Empire State Building. The building can't jump!

Why Don't You?

Characters

FRANKY FRANCINE

SCENE. *Living room. On one side of the room is a box labeled* "TV" *and a chair in front of it. On the other side of the room is a table with a small box on it labeled* "radio."

(FRANCINE *is sitting on a stool, intently listening to the* "radio." FRANKY *enters and stands watching* FRANCINE *for a moment or two.*)

FRANKY: Why do you listen to the radio all the time?

(FRANCINE *turns so that she faces* FRANKY *and the audience.*)

FRANCINE: I want to become a good listener.

FRANKY: Why don't you sit over here? (*Motions to chair in front of "TV."*)

FRANCINE: Why should I sit over there?

FRANKY: In front of the TV you might become a good looker.

What does Francine do? Laugh at Franky and say, "Oh, Franky?" Get mad at Franky and chase him out of the room? Or something else? You decide.

It Had to Be

Characters

SIS MOM TOMMY

SCENE. SIS's *bedroom. A cot is downstage center.*

(SIS *throws back the blanket and sheet and yells. A plastic or paper turtle is lying on top of the bottom sheet.*)

SIS: Mom! Mom! Come here! Quick!

(MOM *rushes in.*)

MOM: What's the matter, Sis? What's the matter?

SIS: Look! Look! (*Points to turtle.*) In my bed!

MOM (*sighing*): I thought you were hurt. Don't yell unless you're hurt.

SIS: But look! There's a turtle in my bed!

MOM: Yes, there is a turtle in your bed. Now, who would put a turtle in your bed?

SIS: Tommy! Who else? It has to be Tommy.

MOM: I suppose so. (*Calls.*) Tommy! Tommy! Come here! Right now!

(TOMMY *enters.*)

TOMMY: What's the matter?

SIS: Matter? There's a turtle in my bed.

TOMMY (*nodding*): I see.

MOM (*seriously*): Tommy, did you put a turtle in Sis's bed?

(TOMMY *nods.*)

MOM: Why did you put a turtle in Sis's bed?

TOMMY (*seriously*): It had to be a turtle, Mom. I couldn't find a frog.

What do Mom and Sis do? Is Mom angry at Tommy? Or does she say, "Oh, Tommy!" and leave the two children glaring at each other? You decide.

Smithtown, U.S.A.

Characters

AUNT SADIE, an old lady CLEM

SCENE. *Bus stop, Smithtown, U.S.A. If it's convenient, put up signs for the names of buildings, or write the names on a chalkboard. Or, say the names of buildings very carefully as you look at them in the skit.*

(AUNT SADIE, *dressed in very plain clothing, is waiting with an old suitcase on each side of her.* CLEM *rushes in.*)

CLEM: Sorry I kept you waiting, Aunt Sadie. Did you have a nice bus trip?

AUNT SADIE: Very nice. My first trip. It was very nice.

CLEM: Welcome to Smithtown, U.S.A. Not much of a town.

AUNT SADIE: Oh, I think it is a very nice town.

CLEM: You can see it all from here. There's the town hall.

AUNT SADIE: Very interesting.

CLEM: There's Laird's Country Store.

AUNT SADIE: Very interesting.

CLEM (*proudly*): And there's Smith Manufacturing Company.

AUNT SADIE: Very, very, very interesting! I know a lot of Smiths, but I didn't know that they were manufactured here!

In the Dumps

Characters

MRS. CRANE MRS. PAYNE

SCENE. *A park.*

(MRS. PAYNE *is sitting on a bench, looking sad and somewhat angry. Enter* MRS. CRANE.)

MRS. CRANE: Good morning, Mrs. Payne. How are you today?

MRS. PAYNE: Terrible! Terrible!

MRS. CRANE: Are you sick?

MRS. PAYNE: No, not sick. Everything's wrong.

MRS. CRANE (*sitting down*): For example? Tell me.

MRS. PAYNE: The basement's flooded. You know?

MRS. CRANE (*nodding*): I know.

MRS. PAYNE: Washing machine broke down. You know?

MRS. CRANE: I know.

MRS. PAYNE: My dog dug up the neighbor's tulips. You know?

MRS. CRANE: I know.

MRS. PAYNE: My son in Akron hasn't written for a month. You know?

MRS. CRANE: I know. You're in the dumps.

MRS. PAYNE: If you felt like me, what would you do?

MRS. CRANE: When I'm in the dumps, I get a new pair of shoes.

(MRS. PAYNE *becomes alert as if she is listening to* MRS. CRANE *for the first time. An idea is flashing through her mind. She looks at* MRS. CRANE'*s shoes.*)

MRS. PAYNE: So—that's where you get your shoes? In the dumps! I've often wondered.

Does Mrs. Crane get mad? Does she shake her head as if saying, you're hopeless? Is Mrs. Payne happier now that she has something besides her troubles to think about? You decide.

The $10,000-Dog

Characters

MOM DAD BILLY

SCENE. *Living room.*

(MOM *and* DAD *are reading newspapers.* BILLY *rushes in.*)

BILLY (*excitedly*): Mom! Dad! I sold Shorty for $10,000!

DAD: What? Sold your dog?

MOM: For $10,000?

DAD: Who bought your dog?

BILLY: Skipper Gertz.

DAD: Billy, come here. (BILLY *stands next to his father's knee, but facing audience.*) You know and I know that Skipper Gertz does not have $10,000.

BILLY: Skipper doesn't need money. We made a trade.

MOM: What trade?

BILLY: I gave him Shorty for $10,000. Skipper gave me his mother cat for $5,000 and five kittens at $1,000 each.

MOM *and* DAD: What?

BILLY: Don't you get it? $5,000 and $5,000 makes $10,000. I sold Shorty for $10,000!

What happens next? You decide.

On Myself

Characters

BEV BUD, her younger brother

SCENE. *Family living room.*

(BUD *is reading.* BEV *rushes in carrying a large sack. The audience can't see the name of the store.*)

BEV: Hi, Bud! Guess what?

BUD: What?

BEV: Mom let me go shopping by myself.

BUD: No questions? No comments? No arguing?

BEV: No arguing. She just said, "Get it, if that's what you want."

BUD: What did you want?

BEV: Guess.

BUD: A dress?

BEV: No.

BUD: Shoes?

BEV: No.

BUD: Slacks?

BEV: No.

BUD: I give up. What did you want?

BEV: I'll show you. (*Opens sack. Takes out roll of wallpaper. Unrolls it a bit and holds it up in front of her.*)

BUD: Wallpaper!

BEV: Yes, wallpaper. I can put it on myself!

BUD: Put it on yourself?

BEV (*nodding*): Yes. Don't you think I can put it on myself?

BUD: I suppose so. But it would look better on the wall!

Does Bev laugh or get mad? You decide.

Touch One

Characters

MOM JENNIFER CHRIS

SCENE. *Left stage is the back porch of the house. Center and right stage are the kitchen of the house. Downstage is a table on which there is a plate holding one cookie.*

(CHRIS *is sitting near the table, chewing as if his mouth is very full.*

MOM *and* JENNIFER *are outside. Each carrying a bag of groceries, they stop at the door.*)

JENNIFER: Are you sure we have enough food for the gang, Mom?

MOM: All set, Jennifer. Besides this food, we have cookies.

JENNIFER: Chocolate chip?

MOM: Chocolate chip. I baked them this morning and put them on a big plate on the kitchen table.

JENNIFER: Oh, good! Here, let me hold your bag.

(MOM *hands bag to* JENNIFER, *gets key out of her purse, pantomimes opening the door. They enter.*)

MOM: Here we are. Hi, Chris!

CHRIS (*still chewing*): Hi!

JENNIFER: Mom, look! (*Points to dish.*)

MOM: Chris, did you eat those cookies?

CHRIS: I didn't touch one.

MOM: Chris, what do you mean? You "didn't touch one"?

CHRIS: Honest, Mom. I didn't touch one. It's still there. (*Points to dish with one cookie.*)

What do Mom and Jennifer do? You decide.

Marked Trail

Characters

ADAM LEON MOM

SCENE. *Home.*

(ADAM *and* LEON *are putting thermos bottles and lunch packages into knapsacks.* MOM *is handing them packages.*)

MOM: Beautiful day for a hike.

ADAM: Great day.

LEON: Just right for walking in the woods.

(ADAM *closes his knapsack and puts it on his back.*)

ADAM: Hurry up, Leon.

MOM: You mustn't keep Mr. Barr waiting. You're lucky to have a friend like Mr. Barr.

LEON: I'm glad he likes to hike. I'm glad he likes the woods. (*Struggles with his knapsack as* MOM *helps him adjust the straps, phone rings.*)

ADAM: I'll get it. (*Answers phone.*) Hello. Oh, Mr. Barr. We're ready. (*Pause.*) What? You can't go today? Oh . . . (*Pause.*) Go without you? (*Pause.*) OK. Guess you're right. Good-bye. (*Hangs up, turns to* MOM *and* LEON.) It was Mr. Barr. (*Walks downstage and stands between* MOM *and* LEON.)

LEON: I know. He can't go.

MOM: What a shame!

ADAM: He said to go without him.

MOM: Without Mr. Barr? You'd get lost in the woods!

ADAM: Oh, no. The trail is marked. The Saturday hikers always mark the trail.

MOM: Mark the trail. How interesting! Just like pioneers and Indians!

ADAM: Not exactly.

MOM: Well, how do the Saturday hikers mark the trail?

ADAM: Oh, they drop candy wrappers, paper tissues, band aids—

LEON: Soda cans—

(MOM *nods that she understands. She may add a few items to the list as the boys call good-bye and exit.*)

A Ship Like This

Characters

MRS. NIFFY
STEWARD
MRS. TIFFY

SCENE. *Aboard an ocean liner. A small table with a chair on either side, is placed downstage, a little left of center.*

(MRS. NIFFY, *who is very unhappy, sits in the right hand chair. She picks up a book, sighs, puts down the book. Looks around. Taps the table with her finger tips. Tries to read again.* MRS. TIFFY *enters left.*)

MRS. TIFFY: Good morning, Mrs. Niffy. How are you today?

MRS. NIFFY: Oh, oh, I just don't know.

MRS. TIFFY: May I sit down?

MRS. NIFFY: Of course! Of course! Do whatever you wish. Anything you do is all right with me.

MRS. TIFFY: Did you sleep well last night?

MRS. NIFFY: No, no, not a wink.

MRS. TIFFY: Were you seasick?

MRS. NIFFY: No, no, I wasn't seasick.

MRS. TIFFY: Well, what's your problem?

MRS. NIFFY: I'm afraid.

MRS. TIFFY: Afraid of what?

MRS. NIFFY: I'm afraid this ship will sink.

MRS. TIFFY: Oh, come now. That's a silly fear. A ship this size doesn't sink.

MRS. NIFFY: Oh, I read about a ship that sank.

MRS. TIFFY: Here comes the steward. Let's talk to him (*or* "her" *if the steward is a woman*).

MRS. NIFFY: All right.

MRS. TIFFY (*speaking to* STEWARD): Pardon me.

STEWARD: Good morning, ladies. May I help you?

MRS. TIFFY: I hope so. We have a question. Maybe you can answer it and put our minds at rest.

STEWARD: I'll answer if I can.

MRS. TIFFY: Does a ship like this sink very often?

STEWARD: Oh, no! (*Women smile happily.*) A ship like this sinks only once.

What do the women do? Do they take the Steward seriously? Does Mrs. Niffy panic as Mrs. Tiffy tries to comfort her? Or are they disgusted? You decide.

Funny-Bone Plays

A play, unlike a skit, has a plot, a story line that players act out. Although the characters in a funny-bone play are often comic because they are silly, they are more like real people than characters in a skit. When you play a part, try to understand the character you represent. Then try to feel, talk, and act like him. Never drop out of character and be yourself, not even for a moment.

If the audience laughs loudly during the play, pause for a moment but stay in character. When it is quiet enough for the audience to hear the next line, go on with the play.

Pantomime, that is, acting without words, is very important. Sometimes the expression on your face or the movement of your body will tell more about how you feel than spoken lines.

Actors in a play must work together as a team. They must have one idea: to act out the story in such a way that the audience can hear the lines, understand the plot, and react to the situation. Each actor must not only know his own lines and be able to say them clearly, he must also know the play as a whole so well that he can react to the lines and actions of other actors and so keep the play moving towards its climax, the high point of the plot.

Practice your funny-bone play until you feel like the characters in it. Then act out the story with gusto for an audience.

My Treasure

Characters

FIRST SERVANT	SECOND SERVANT
MERCHANT	Several OTHER SERVANTS

SCENE. *A marketplace in Persia, long ago. A little to the left of center downstage is a chair or a big inverted carton labeled,* "camel." *Beside it and on top of it are several large brown bags, either painted to look like leather bags or labeled,* "leather bags." *In the bags are various kinds of fabrics. Old bedspreads, discarded drapes, or bright clothing will give the desired impression. Each character wears a cloak, draped like a burnous.*

(*As the scene opens,* MERCHANT *looks in a bag, smiles, closes the bag.* SERVANTS *watch.*)

FIRST SERVANT: Master, your buying trip was successful.

MERCHANT (*standing straight*): Very, very successful! Such silks! Such tapestries! Such brocades! And at such low prices! I'll make a fortune! (SERVANTS *nod.*) However, I do have a problem.

FIRST SERVANT: Problem? What problem?

MERCHANT: I was too successful. I bought too much material. One camel cannot carry this load.

FIRST SERVANT: What can you do?

MERCHANT: Buy another camel. (SERVANTS *nod.*) Wait here. Guard my treasure well while I'm away.

SERVANTS: Yes, Master, we'll guard your treasure well!

(MERCHANT *turns to go, looks at sky.*)

MERCHANT: Mmmmm. I think I see a rain cloud. (SERVANTS *look at cloud.*) It might rain.

SERVANTS: Yes, it might rain.

MERCHANT: Now, if it starts to rain, cover the leather bags. The bags hold expensive cloth. Be sure to cover the leather bags!

FIRST SERVANT: Yes, sir! If it rains, we'll cover the leather bags!

OTHER SERVANTS: We'll cover the leather bags.

MERCHANT: Good-bye for now.

SERVANTS: Good-bye.

(MERCHANT *exits.*)

FIRST SERVANT (*looking again at sky*): Look! It's going to rain. (*Holds out hand.*) It is raining! I feel rain!

OTHER SERVANTS (*babble*): Me, too. I feel rain. I'm getting wet.

SECOND SERVANT (*speaking above babble*): What'll we do?

FIRST SERVANT: Master said, "Cover the leather bags." But with what?

SECOND SERVANT: With our cloaks.

FIRST SERVANT: No, no! We'd get wet.

OTHER SERVANTS: That's right! We'd get wet!

FIRST SERVANT: I know. I have an idea.

OTHER SERVANTS: What?

FIRST SERVANT: Master said, "Don't let the bags get wet."

SECOND SERVANT: What'll we do? Don't stand and talk!

FIRST SERVANT: All right, I'll show you. Stand around. All around. (*Points to* SECOND SERVANT.) You help me. Spread out your cloaks. That's it.

(*As* FIRST SERVANT *is giving directions,* OTHER SERVANTS *form a semicircle with back to the audience. They spread out their cloaks so no one can see what* FIRST *and* SECOND SERVANTS *are doing. They encourage* FIRST SERVANT *with remarks.* "Good!" "That's it" *and at the same time pantomime getting wet by shaking their heads, shrugging shoulders, shaking selves.*

Only the OTHER SERVANTS *can see that* FIRST *and* SECOND SERVANTS *are taking cloth out of the bags and covering the bags with* MERCHANT'*s treasured fabric.*

MERCHANT, *with cloak thrown over his head to protect himself from the rain, enters.* FIRST SERVANT *runs to meet him. Other* SERVANTS *remain in front of hidden bags now covered with fabric.*)

FIRST SERVANT: Master, did you get the camel?

MERCHANT (*not looking up*): Yes, I got the camel. A man will deliver him when the rain stops. Don't stop me. I'm worried about my bags!

FIRST SERVANT: Don't worry! We covered the leather bags.

(MERCHANT, *head lowered, continues to walk toward camel.*)

MERCHANT: Good! Good!

FIRST SERVANT: Look Master! (SERVANTS *step aside so everyone can see bags covered with fabrics.*) See! We covered the leather bags!

(MERCHANT *looks up. Sees fabrics spread on bags.*)

MERCHANT (*gasping*): My treasure!

(MERCHANT *walks in front of* SERVANTS *to a bag, feels a piece of wet fabric, holds it up.*)

MERCHANT: My soggy treasure! (*Throws a piece of wet fabric over his head.*) You covered the bags, but what about my treasure? (*Slumps down, wailing.*) My treasure! My ruined treasure!

Seven Simons

Characters

FIRST SIMON
SECOND SIMON
OTHER SIMONS
STRANGER

SCENE. *Bank along an imaginary river that appears to be upstage. Every Simon wears a hat and carries a fishing pole, a long stick with a dangling line. Tie a weight or a cork on each line, but do not use hooks.*

(FIRST SIMON *pantomimes wading and then stepping out of the river center stage. He dries the soles of his feet on the grass, rubs the top of his feet on his pants, blows on his feet. He feels them to see if they are dry, seems to be satisfied, then walks downstage center and calls to other* SIMONS.)

FIRST SIMON: Yo, ho! Time to go! (*Motions to other* SIMONS *to join him.*)

(*They enter from each side of the stage, wade in the river, and one by one step onto the bank and join the* First Simon *downstage.*)

First Simon: Ah, here we are. It was a great day for fishing.

Second Simon: But I didn't catch any fish.

Third Simon: I didn't catch any fish.

Other Simons: Nor I. Nor I. Nor I. Nor I.

First Simon: I just said, "It was a great day for fishing." Nothing wrong with the day.

Other Simons: No, no. Nothing wrong with the day.

First Simon: Now, it's time to go home.

(Other Simons *look at the sun and nod.*)

Other Simons (*nodding*): Time to go home. Time to go home.

First Simon: Wait. We better think before we go.

Other Simons (*nodding*): Better think before we go.

First Simon: It was a great day for fishing.

Other Simons: Great day.

First Simon: But fishing can be dangerous.

Other Simons: Very dangerous.

First Simon: One of us might have drowned.

Other Simons (*excited*): Drowned? Who? Who? Who drowned?

First Simon (*yelling*): Quiet! (Others *calm down.*) I said, "Someone *might* have drowned." We better think.

Other Simons: Better think.

FIRST SIMON: There were seven Simons when we left this morning.

OTHER SIMONS: Yes, seven Simons.

FIRST SIMON: We'll count. If we count seven Simons here, we'll know that no one drowned. Let's count.

OTHER SIMONS: Let's count. (OTHER SIMONS *stand in a straight line.*)

(FIRST SIMON *counts out loud as he points to each Simon. He forgets to count himself.*)

FIRST SIMON: One, two, three, four, five, six. Six Simons! One Simon drowned!

SECOND SIMON: Let me count.

(FIRST SIMON *gets in line.* SECOND SIMON *points to each*

one in line as he counts out loud and forgets to count himself.)

SECOND SIMON: One, two, three, four, five, six—six Simons! One Simon drowned.

(OTHER SIMONS *all count out loud, as they get out of line, and point to each other. Each forgets to count himself. Each yells,* "Six Simons! One Simon drowned!" *They work themselves into a frenzy. They go to the river calling,* "Simon! Simon!" *They prance up and down the stage yelling,* "Simon! Simon!"

STRANGER *enters. Stands a little left of center downstage. Looks at the* SIMONS. STRANGER *shakes his head, much puzzled.* FIRST SIMON *notices* STRANGER *and rushes downstage to talk to him.)*

FIRST SIMON: Sir! Sir! (OTHER SIMONS *rush downstage.)*

STRANGER: What's wrong?

FIRST SIMON: One Simon drowned. Did you see him?

OTHER SIMONS (*together*): We lost a Simon! One Simon's missing! One Simon drowned!

STRANGER: Just a minute. Calm down. Tell me the story.

FIRST SIMON: We are seven Simons. This morning we came fishing. (*After each sentence,* OTHER SIMONS *nod in agreement.* STRANGER *nods that he understands.*) We fished until it was time to go home. Fishing can be dangerous. A person can drown. So we lined up and counted ourselves. Each time we counted, we found only six Simons.

OTHER SIMONS (*together*): Six Simons. I counted. I counted.

FIRST SIMON: There were seven Simons this morning. Now we count six Simons. So one Simon must have drowned.

(STRANGER *looks at* SIMONS. *Points to each one. Quickly counts silently.*)

STRANGER: You're sure that you counted.

SIMONS: Yes, yes, we counted.

STRANGER: Everyone counted six Simons.

SIMONS: Yes, yes! Six Simons.

STRANGER: Are you sure one Simon drowned? Did you see him fall into the water?

FIRST SIMON: No! No! Nothing like that. We know that one Simon is missing. This morning we were seven Simons. Now we count six Simons. One Simon must be missing!

STRANGER: Maybe I can help you find your missing Simon.

SIMONS (*together*): How? Tell us!

STRANGER: All right. Line up. (SIMONS *line up.*) Everyone, put your hat on the ground in front of you. (*Each* SIMON *does so.*) Now, we'll count hats. Altogether. (STRANGER *points to each hat as he and* SIMONS *count together.*) One, two, three, four, five, six, seven!

SIMONS: Seven hats!

STRANGER: Now! Everyone, pick up your hat. (*Each does so.*) Put your hat on your head. (*Each does so.*) We'll count again. Altogether. One, two, three, four, five six, seven! There are seven hats on seven heads. There must be seven Simons!

SIMONS (*yelling*): Seven Simons! Seven Simons!

(*They crowd around* STRANGER, *but do not get in front of him.* FIRST SIMON *extends his right hand to* STRANGER *and pumps arm up and down as he thanks him.* OTHER SIMONS *are happy but quiet.*)

FIRST SIMON: Thank you! Thank you! Thank you! You found our missing Simon! Thank you!

STRANGER: You are welcome. Very welcome! (*He gets weary with the handshaking.*)

FIRST SIMON: If you need help, remember the seven Simons.

STRANGER: Oh, I'll remember the seven Simons! Now, I must say good-bye and be on my way. (*Exits.*)

(*Seven* SIMONS *call and wave as* STRANGER *exits.*)

SIMONS: Good-bye, our friend. Good-bye. (*They pick up their fishing rods, form a line, and march off the stage counting.*)

SIMONS: One, two, three, four, five, six, seven. One, two———

The basic story on which this play is based has many versions. In* "The Men from Gotham," *there are twelve silly men. In a play, counting to eleven over and over again would slow down the action. If, however, there are more or less than eight actors who want to be in this play, you can have five, six, or eight Simons and change the lines accordingly.

Shut the Door!

Characters

HUSBAND	FIRST THIEF
WIFE	SECOND THIEF

SCENE. *Home of a shopkeeper in Europe long ago. There are two exits. Exit right leads to the kitchen. Exit left leads to outdoors. Two blocks of wood are placed at this exit, but behind scene. At the end of the play,* WIFE *bangs them together to make the sound of door being slammed.*

Downstage center is a dining table set for two with a pretty, unbreakable vase in the center, a covered dish at the left end of the table, and a basket of rolls at the right end. There's a chair at each end of the table.

On chests and small tables around the room are various pretty knickknacks such as candlesticks, picture in frame, vases, and so on.

HUSBAND *is wearing a suit with a vest. The vest pocket looks as if it might hold a watch.* WIFE *is wearing a dress and apron and looks as if she has been cleaning, washing, and cooking all day. However, she does wear a necklace. It must be easy to remove.*

(*As the scene opens,* HUSBAND *is sitting at the left end of the table, glowering at the covered dish.* WIFE *stands waiting for him to speak. He takes the lid from the dish, looks inside, smells the food, feels outside of dish, replaces lid on dish and yells.*)

HUSBAND: Mmmmm! Meat pie! Cold! Take that dish back to the kitchen! Warm it up! It's cold!

WIFE: I worked half a day on that meat pie. I say it is good meat pie.

HUSBAND: I say it's a cold meat pie. Take it back to the kitchen! (WIFE *picks up dish and goes to kitchen. He continues to talk.*) I slave all day in the shop.

(WIFE *returns without dish, but in one hand she carries a rolling pin that she waves as she answers.*)

WIFE: I slave all day in the house. (*Puts rolling pin on table, sits down.*)

HUSBAND: When I get home, I find a cold supper. A cold house.

WIFE: It's a clean house.

HUSBAND: It's a cold house.

WIFE: A cold house? No wonder. You left the door open.

HUSBAND (*turning in seat*): The door *is* open. Shut the door.

WIFE (*yelling*): *You* shut the door!

HUSBAND (*very angry*): You shut the door!

WIFE: You shut the door!

HUSBAND: I say, you shut the door!

WIFE: I say, you shut the door!

HUSBAND: Wait a minute. Yelling is silly. (*She nods.*) You always argue. (*She shrugs her shoulders and points to herself as if saying,* "I argue?") You always have the last word. (*She nods.*) We'll settle this argument quietly. We'll make a bargain.

WIFE: What bargain?

HUSBAND: The first person who speaks will shut the door.

(WIFE *starts to answer but doesn't make a sound, puts her hand over her mouth. Then she folds her arms over her chest and stares at her husband.* HUSBAND *folds his arms over his chest and stares at his wife.*)

FIRST THIEF (*outside*): Hey! The door's open.

SECOND THIEF: Don't hear anything.

FIRST THIEF: Maybe no one's home. Let's go in. (THIEVES *enter, drop bags near door.*)

SECOND THIEF (*going to* HUSBAND): Pardon me, we lost our way. (*Neither* HUSBAND *nor* WIFE *moves or speaks.*) Could you tell us how to get to Roundtree Place? (*No one answers.* THIEVES *gesture to each other as if saying,* "What goes on?")

FIRST THIEF (*addressing* WIFE): Excuse me, do you know where Mr. Farly lives? (*no answer*) Hope you don't mind our stepping in.

(*No answer, no movement.*)

FIRST THIEF: Think they're real?

SECOND THIEF: I think they're real.

FIRST THIEF: Think they're dead?

SECOND THIEF: No, I don't think they're dead.

FIRST THIEF: Think they'd mind if we look around?

SECOND THIEF: No. I don't think they'd mind if we look around.

(FIRST THIEF *picks up bags and hands one to* SECOND THIEF. *They work on opposite sides of stage, quickly picking up objects and putting them into their bags. Neither* HUSBAND *nor* WIFE *moves or speaks.*)

FIRST THIEF: Nice candlestick. (*Puts it in his bag.*)

SECOND THIEF: Good quality vase. (*Puts it in his bag.*)

FIRST THIEF (*holding up picture in frame*): Think this would sell?

SECOND THIEF: Frame might. Try it.

(FIRST THIEF *puts frame in his bag. Both come to table. No one moves or makes a sound.*)

SECOND THIEF: I like this vase. (*Reaches between couple to pick up vase, puts it in his bag.*)

FIRST THIEF (*holding up fork*): Good quality silver.

(*They scoop up silver, put it in bags.*)

SECOND THIEF (*standing behind* WIFE): Think this necklace is genuine?

FIRST THIEF: Take it and see. (SECOND THIEF *removes necklace, puts it in bag.* WIFE *doesn't move.* THIEF *steps back to look around room.*)

FIRST THIEF: Wonder what kind of watch he is wearing.

SECOND THIEF: Look and see.

(FIRST THIEF *starts to remove watch.* HUSBAND *doesn't move.* WIFE *suddenly picks up rolling pin, raises it, and yells.*)

WIFE: Stop! Leave him alone. (THIEVES *stare.* HUSBAND *doesn't move.*) Stop! He's my husband! Leave him alone! Get out! Get out! Drop those bags! Get out!

(THIEVES *drop bags as* WIFE *starts to come after them with raised rolling pin. Thieves exit on the run.* HUSBAND *doesn't move or speak.* WIFE *returns to her place at the table. Remains standing, stares at her husband who doesn't move, and at last speaks.*)

WIFE: What do you think of that? (*no answer*) What do you have to say about that?

HUSBAND (*without emotion*): You spoke first. Shut the door!

(WIFE *stamps across the stage, exits left. Offstage she knocks two pieces of wood together to make sound of door being slammed. He smiles, self-satisfied, and reaches for a roll. He breaks the roll in two and starts to eat.*)

(CURTAIN)

Fit for a King

Characters

KING GOBBO   QUEEN AMELIA

SERVANTS	PAGE	LORD OF EXCHEQUER
	LORD CHAMBERLAIN	KITCHEN BOY
	COOK	TASTER
	MAID	MAJORDOMO

SCENE. *Dining hall in the palace of King Gobbo of Gloomytoo. The table, set for two, is placed center downstage with two chairs behind it.*

(MAID *is adjusting the silverware as* QUEEN *and* MAJORDOMO *watch. Other* SERVANTS, *except* KITCHEN BOY, *stand upstage at attention.*)

QUEEN: Is that knife perfectly straight?

(MAJORDOMO *leans until his eyes are on a level with the table top. He closes one eye and squints and then stands up straight.*)

MAJORDOMO: I think the knife leans slightly this way. (*Motions to one side.* MAID *adjusts knife.*) Just slightly. Slightly! (*He again leans over to judge the perfection of the placement of the knife, stands up straight.*) I think that's it. A table fit for a king.

QUEEN: Oh, I do hope so. At least I hope that His Majesty will think that the table is fit for a king.

MAID: Yet, you wonder. Don't you?

QUEEN: No, I don't wonder. I know.

MAJORDOMO (*to* MAID): She knows that the king will complain.

(*All other* SERVANTS *nod.*)

MAID: Why?

MAJORDOMO: Because the King always complains.

(*Other* SERVANTS *nod.*)

QUEEN: Maybe the King won't complain today.

MAJORDOMO: Why not today?

QUEEN: Because today is the third Friday of April. (*Name the day and month that the play is being given.*) Maybe, just maybe he'll be in good humor on the third Friday in April. Maybe he won't complain.

(LORD CHAMBERLAIN *steps forward.*)

LORD CHAMBERLAIN: Poor Queen, you always hope that each new day may be a special day. (QUEEN *nods.*) At least the affairs of the King are in order.

(LORD OF EXCHEQUER, *holding large book and bag of candy money, steps forward.*)

LORD OF EXCHEQUER: All the gold has been counted before dinner.

(COOK *steps forward.*)

COOK: Dinner is cooked to perfection.

(TASTER *steps forward.*)

TASTER: The dinner is delicious. I tasted it. No poison.

MAID: The table is set to perfection.

MAJORDOMO: Everything is in order. Everything is fit for a king!

(PAGE *blows a bugle if he has one. Otherwise he beats a drum, rings a bell, or blows a whistle to announce the entrance of the* KING.)

PAGE: Behold! His Majesty, King Gobbo of Gloomytoo.

(MAJORDOMO *goes to door to usher in* KING *who enters with great strides.* SERVANTS *bow from waist.* QUEEN *curtsies.*)

QUEEN and SERVANTS (*speaking together*): Good day, Your Majesty.

KING (*yelling*): Is that the way to greet a king?

(COOK *and* PAGE *exit.* MAJORDOMO *steps forward.*)

MAJORDOMO: Yes, Your Majesty. In the *Book of Court Etiquette*, page 1,652, Paragraph G, it states, "The proper way to greet a king is to say: Good day, Your Majesty."

KING: Is that a greeting fit for a king?

MAJORDOMO: Yes, sir. It says so in the book.

KING: Then find another book! Get out of my sight! Get out of my kingdom.

(KING *sits down, looks at table.*)

KING: Maid! (MAID *steps forward.*) Is this table setting fit for a king?

MAID: Yes. sir. In the *Book of Palace Management,* it says

KING: If that's what it says, get another book. Get out of my sight. Get out of my kingdom!

KING: Where's my food? (PAGE *enters carrying soup for two, serves* KING *and then* QUEEN.) Has this soup been tasted?

(TASTER *steps forward.*)

TASTER: Oh, yes, Your Majesty. The soup is delicious! No poison!

(KING *tastes soup.*)

KING: You call that soup fit for a king? Get out of my sight! Get out of my kingdom! (*Notices* PAGE.) You, too. On your way out, tell the cook to bring the rest of my dinner.

(COOK *enters with covered dish.* KING *lifts lid, smells food.*)

KING: You call that a dinner fit for a king? (COOK *nods.*) Get out of my sight. Get out of my kingdom!

(KING *notices* QUEEN.)

KING: Amelia! Why are you wearing yellow? (*Name whatever color* QUEEN *is wearing.*) You know I hate yellow!

QUEEN: Your Majesty———

KING: And why did you sing at 7:18 this morning? You know I always rise at 7:19.

QUEEN: Your Majesty———

KING: And why aren't you eating? Take this food to your parlor. Eat there.

(QUEEN *picks up dish of food.*)

QUEEN: Yes, Your Majesty. (*Starts to exit.*)

LORD CHAMBERLAIN (*to* QUEEN): May I help you, Your Majesty?

KING (*to* LORD CHAMBERLAIN): If that's all you have to do —carry food—get out of my sight! Get out of my kingdom!

(QUEEN *and* LORD CHAMBERLAIN *exit.* KING *looks at table.*)

KING: Nothing to eat. Guess I'll count my money. Lord of Exchequer, bring me my money. I want to count it.

LORD OF EXCHEQUER: Here is your money, sir. It's all counted.

KING: I want to count it myself.

LORD OF EXCHEQUER: Excuse me, Your Majesty, but your arithmetic, sir———

KING: My arithmetic. Who questions my arithmetic? Get out of my sight! Get out of my kingdom!

(KING *starts to count money as* LORD OF EXCHEQUER *exits.* QUEEN *enters and stands unnoticed upstage.*)

KING: Now 5 and 7 are 19 and 6 are 22 and 3 are 30. Now I'll check. (*Starts to count coins one by one.*) Oh, it doesn't come out right.

QUEEN (*stepping forward*): Gobbo, may I help you?

KING: You, a woman! Help me! With my arithmetic! How dare you think of such a thing? Get out of my sight! Get out of my kingdom!

(QUEEN *runs off the stage.* KING *opens his treasury book and looks at it.*)

KING: Oh, dear, I can't add. Lord of Exchequer! (*Silence.*) That's right. I told him to go. I'm hungry. Cook! (*Silence.*) That's right. I told her to go. In fact I told all the servants to go. Amelia! Amelia! (*Silence.*) I told her to go. (*Suddenly* KING *is very sad.*) I'm alone. I'm hungry. I'm the saddest king in the whole wide world. In fact, I'm the saddest person in the whole wide world. And all because I complain. What will I do?

(KITCHEN BOY *enters on tiptoe.* KING *looks up.*)

KING (*cheerfully*): Hello, there! Hello!

KITCHEN BOY: I'm sorry, Your Majesty. I'm getting out as fast as I can.

KING: Wait! Please wait! (BOY *stops.*) Can you cook something? Anything?

KITCHEN BOY: Yes, indeed, Your Majesty. I've been your kitchen boy for seven years.

KING: Great! Wonderful! Excellent! What can you cook for me now? Right now?

KITCHEN BOY: Well, sir, it's not a dish fit for a king.

KING: A dish fit for a king? Any pure food is fit for a king. That is, a hungry king. Right now I am a hungry king!

KITCHEN BOY: There are some boiled potatoes in the kitchen. They were cooked for the servants.

KING: Bring me boiled potatoes!

KITCHEN BOY: They aren't peeled. They have the jackets on.

KING: So what? I'll learn to peel a potato.

KITCHEN BOY: I am sure you can learn, sir. (*Exits quickly and returns as quickly as possible with a dish of boiled potatoes with the jackets on.*)

(KING *muses while alone.*)

KING: A boiled potato. A plain boiled potato. I wonder what it tastes like. (*Sees* KITCHEN BOY *returning.*) Sit down. (*Motions to* QUEEN's *chair.*) The Queen won't mind if you sit here.

(KITCHEN BOY *sits down.*)

KING: Now, what do we do?

KITCHEN BOY: You stab the potato, thus. (*He puts fork into a potato, holds it up.* KING *follows action.*) Then you peel thus. (*King copies action but stops with partly peeled potato to taste it.*) Say, this is delicious! Marvelous! Wonderful! This is a dish fit for a king! Wait until I tell Amelia! (*Calls.*) Amelia! Amelia! Oh, I forgot. She's gone. They are all gone.

KITCHEN BOY: I can get them, sir. They are at the gate.

KING: Go! Go! Go! Get them all! Tell them to come here. I have news. I have good news for them.

KITCHEN BOY: Yes, sir! Yes, sir! (*Runs off the stage.*)

(KING *takes another bite, chews slowly, greatly pleased, pantomimes his delight. He must not have any food in his mouth when it is time to speak.* QUEEN *and* SERVANTS *enter.* KING *rises.* QUEEN *stands at her place behind table.* SERVANTS *stand beside* KING *and* QUEEN *forming a semicircle with royalty in the center.* KING *throws his arms wide in gesture of welcome as others are returning.*)

KING: Hello! Hello! Hello! Everyone, welcome! Welcome! (*He continues his welcome until everyone is in place.*) I have good news for you. I've learned a lesson. (QUEEN *and* SERVANTS *look surprised.*) I am going to change my ways. (QUEEN *and* SERVANTS *gasp with delight, but don't make a sound.*) I'm not going to complain anymore! (QUEEN *and* SERVANTS *cheer.*) I've discovered a dish fit for a king. (QUEEN *and* SERVANTS *cheer more loudly. King holds up boiled potato on a fork.*) I have discovered the boiled potato. (QUEEN *and* SERVANTS *stare silently.*) From now on, I and my household will eat boiled potatoes. (QUEEN *and* SERVANTS *nod.*) Nothing but boiled potatoes. (QUEEN *and* SERVANTS *look startled.*) Breakfast, lunch, and dinner. Boiled potatoes! A dish fit for a king.

(QUEEN *and* SERVANTS *faint.* KING *pays no attention to them. He continues to hold up the boiled potato on a fork.*)

(CURTAIN)

If you wish to put this play on with fewer characters, combine the roles of some of the servants and change the lines accordingly.

Why Catch a Leprechaun?

Characters

ANNOUNCER
HEAD LEPRECHAUN
FIRST LEPRECHAUN
OTHER LEPRECHAUNS
TOM FITZPATRICK

SCENE. *A bare field in Ireland. Announcer stands before curtain.*

ANNOUNCER: The Leprechauns in our play are child-size. In all other ways they are very much like the mischievous elves of Ireland. Our scene is forty acres of bare Irish soil. (*Exits.*)

(*Curtain opens. If there is no curtain, the* LEPRECHAUNS *troop in merrily. Each* LEPRECHAUN *wears four red garters—one on each arm and one on each leg. A lively Irish tune is played softly offstage.* LEPRECHAUNS *play their own version of follow-the-leader in time to music.* HEAD LEPRECHAUN *comes downstage, a little to the right of center. Other* LEPRECHAUNS *follow his every motion and command. Then, other* LEPRECHAUNS *move about,* HEAD LEPRECHAUN *stays in one spot. He moves in time to the music. He may start with an Irish jig, then do exercises with his arms and legs, or give a command,*

"Tumble all!" *as others turn somersaults, play leapfrog, or leap about the stage. Into their midst, not observed, creeps* TOM FITZPATRICK, *a rope in his hand. He sneaks up behind* HEAD LEPRECHAUN *and slips a rope around his waist. Music stops.*)

TOM: I got you! I got you!

HEAD LEPRECHAUN: You got me, Tom Fitzpatrick, and what will you do with me now?

(TOM *holds onto the rope, but comes around to the side of* HEAD LEPRECHAUN.)

TOM: I'll hold onto you.

HEAD LEPRECHAUN: Hold onto me? Now, isn't that a foolish waste of time? Tom Fitzpatrick, you surprise me. (TOM *nods as if saying,* "I know I surprised you.") You should be home minding your father's cows. Here you are standing, holding onto a poor little Leprechaun. And what was the Leprechaun doing? Nothing, but dancing to an Irish tune. Does an Irish tune disturb you, Tom? Have you no love for an Irish tune?

TOM: Oh, I like an Irish tune, all right. I also like Irish gold.

HEAD LEPRECHAUN: Oh, do you like Irish gold?

TOM: I do like Irish gold. And I know that you know where I can find a pot of Irish gold. It's buried in this field, or else you wouldn't be dancing here.

HEAD LEPRECHAUN: You know a lot, Tom Fitzpatrick. What else do you know?

TOM: I know I won't let you go until you show me the spot where the pot of gold is buried.

HEAD LEPRECHAUN: And if I tell you, what then?

TOM: I'll let you go.

HEAD LEPRECHAUN: What more? What more do you promise, Tom Fitzpatrick?

TOM: I promise—(*Thinks a moment.*) Never again will I try to catch a Leprechaun.

HEAD LEPRECHAUN: You promise, Tom Fitzpatrick?

TOM: I promise.

HEAD LEPRECHAUN: It's a bargain. I'll show you the spot where the pot of gold is hidden. You promise never to catch a Leprechaun again.

TOM (*raising right hand*): I promise.

HEAD LEPRECHAUN: Then let me see. (*Music is played softly offstage.*

HEAD LEPRECHAUN *goes slowly and mysteriously around the stage, as if feeling with his foot, leaning over as if listening to sounds from within the earth.* TOM *follows, still hanging onto the rope around* HEAD LEPRECHAUN'S *waist, and acting as if he can't quite figure out what* HEAD LEPRECHAUN *is doing. Other* LEPRECHAUNS *watch closely. At last,* HEAD LEPRECHAUN *comes back to the place where he started.*)

HEAD LEPRECHAUN: Here. (*Music stops.*)

TOM: This is where you started.

HEAD LEPRECHAUN: Of course! I always dance on top of my pot of gold.

TOM: How can I get the gold?

HEAD LEPRECHAUN: Dig six feet down.

TOM: Dig? With what?

HEAD LEPRECHAUN: Now, that's your problem.

TOM: I need a spade. If I leave this spot, I'll never find it again without you. You'll have to come home with me. (*Starts to drag* HEAD LEPRECHAUN.)

HEAD LEPRECHAUN: Oh no, you don't do that. You promised to let me go when I showed you the spot.

TOM: I know I promised. And a promise is a promise. But every inch of this field looks like the next. If I go home and get a spade, how will I find the spot when I come back? (HEAD LEPRECHAUN *shrugs his shoulders as if saying,* "I don't know." TOM *thinks.*) I know. Take off a red garter. (HEAD LEPRECHAUN *does so.*) Now I'll mark the spot with this red garter. Now do you promise not to move the garter that marks the spot above the gold?

HEAD LEPRECHAUN (*raising right hand*): I promise.

(TOM *removes rope from* HEAD LEPRECHAUN.)

TOM: Remember, you promised not to move that red garter! (HEAD LEPRECHAUN *raises hand again.*) Good-bye, little man. I'll soon be back with my spade to get my gold. (*Exits.*)

(*Other* LEPRECHAUNS *rush downstage, excited and worried.*)

FIRST LEPRECHAUN: You told him. You told him where to find the pot of gold.

HEAD LEPRECHAUN: He caught me. I had to tell him.

FIRST LEPRECHAUN: And you promised not to move your garter.

HEAD LEPRECHAUN: I promised not to move the garter, and a promise is a promise.

FIRST LEPRECHAUN: What will we do now?

OTHER LEPRECHAUNS (*weeping*): What will we do now?

HEAD LEPRECHAUN: Use your wits, my lads.

OTHER LEPRECHAUNS: How?

HEAD LEPRECHAUN: What marks the spot?

OTHER LEPRECHAUNS: A red garter.

HEAD LEPRECHAUN: And how many garters does each of you have?

FIRST LEPRECHAUN: Two on the legs and two on the sleeves.

HEAD LEPRECHAUN: And that makes?

FIRST LEPRECHAUN: Four for each.

HEAD LEPRECHAUN: Correct! Now this is the plan. Don't move this garter. I made a promise, and a promise is a promise. But sprinkle red garters all over the forty acres.

(OTHER LEPRECHAUNS *are delighted. Each shouts whatever comes to his mind:* "I get it!" "Let's do it!" "Hurry up!" *The* LEPRECHAUNS *quickly spread red garters about the stage.* Tom *re-enters, waving spade.* Leprechauns *scamper upstage.*)

Tom (*yelling happily*): I got it! I got it! I got my spade. Now to get my pot of gold! Beneath the red garter. (*Stops center downstage and for the first time looks around.*) Red garter! Which red garter?

(Head Leprechaun *runs downstage, teasing* Tom, *but not getting close to him*).

Head Leprechaun: That's for us to know and you to find out.

(Tom *drops spade and starts to chase* Head Leprechaun.)

Tom: You, you, Leprechaun!

(Head Leprechaun *dodges. He and* Other Leprechauns *chant,* "You promised! You promised!" Tom *gives up chase quickly. Picks up his spade and leans on it. Speaks slowly, as if thinking hard, out loud.*)

Tom: I know. I promised not to catch a Leprechaun. And why not promise? Who wants to catch a Leprechaun? He'll fool you every time!

(Tom *puts spade on shoulder and stamps off the stage. Irish music starts again.* Leprechauns *start to jig, singing in time to the music,* "He promised. He promised. He promised. He promised.")

(Curtain)

(*If there is no curtain* Leprechuans *dance off the stage as they sing.*)

A Few Stage Terms

AD LIB: to make up lines or add words on the spur of the moment

CLIMAX: highest point of dramatic tension in skit or play

CUE: a speech or action that serves as a signal for another actor to speak or act

DEAD PAN: no expression on face

DIALOGUE: conversation in play

DOWNSTAGE: the part of the stage nearest the audience

LEAD LINE: line that must be emphasized if the audience is to understand a joke

LEFT STAGE: the part of the stage on the actors' left when they are facing the audience

OFFSTAGE: behind the scenes

ONSTAGE: the area which the audience sees

PANTOMIME: acting silently, portraying a situation or an attitude with bodily movements and facial expression

PUNCH LINE: the line in the joke, skit, or play that makes the point

RIGHT STAGE: the part of the stage on the actors' right when they are facing the audience

UPSTAGE: the part of the stage farthest from the audience

Other Books to Help You

After you have used the riddles, jokes, skits, and plays in this book, you may want to make up your own funny-bone dramatics. You may want to make your own puppets to use with material in this book, or other material of your own choosing. The following books will help you.

Bruce, Dana. *Tell Me a Joke.* Platt and Munk, 1966.

Carlson, Bernice Wells. *Act It Out.* Abingdon Press, 1956.

———. *Do It Yourself.* Abingdon Press, 1952.

———. *The Right Play for You.* Abingdon, 1960.

Cerf, Bennett. *Bennett Cerf's Book of Riddles.* Random House, 1960.

Chrystie F. N. *The First Book of Jokes and Funny Things.* Franklin Watts, 1951.

———. *Riddle Me This.* Oxford University Press, 1940.

Fenner, P. R. *Fools and Funny Fellows:* More Time to Laugh Tales. Alfred A. Knopf, 1947.

Fox, Sonny. *Funnier Than the First One.* G. P. Putnam's Sons, 1972.

———. *Jokes and How to Tell Them.* G. P. Putnam's Sons, 1965.

Gilbreath, A. T. *Beginning to Read Riddles and Jokes.* Follett, 1967.

Hake, Helen, *The Big Book of Jokes.* Franklin Watts, 1971.

Jagendorf, Moritz. *Noodlehead Stories From Around the World.* Vanguard Press, 1957.

———. *Puppets for Beginners.* Plays, Inc., 1952.

Kohl, M. *Jokes for Children.* Hill & Wang, 1963.

Lewis, Shari. *Making Easy Puppets.* E. P. Dutton, 1958.

Ross, Laura and Frank, Jr., *Finger Puppets.* Lothrop Lee & Shepard, 1971.

Tichenor, Tom. *Tom Tichenor's Puppets.* Abingdon Press, 1971.

Index